ANDAMAN TOUR OF 2016

WRITTEN BY: - ARINDAM SAIN

****

Episode: - 01

Location: Kunchuberia Branch, Allahabad Bank

Sumon (Branch Manager):- ***Your LFC for 4 (Four) Years Block from 01.06.2012 to 31.05.2016 is going to expire on 31.05.2016. You utilize the LFC Block now in this winter season. Go for a long tour with your wife.***

Sadhan (Sub-Staff of that Branch):- ***Yes, Arindam ! Go for any tour in this winter season only. Any tour in summer season is not a feasible decision at all unless you are going for a tour in hill stations only.***

Arindam (Officer of that Branch):- ***Yeah! I know that, but, I am confused now. Where to go? Bhutan! Rajasthan! Kerala! Manali! or Goa! ? I am still confused.***

*Sumon :- **Go for Goa!***

*Sadhan :- **No! Sir! There is a better alternative than Goa! Last year, I visited Andaman. Go for Andaman! That's a better place than Goa. In any case, in our Allahabad Bank, each and every employee is eligible to get the flight fare of economy class for self as well as for his/her dependant/s for going for a tour to Andaman & Nicobar Islands by flight.***

*Sumon :- **This offer is only for Andaman Tour. For travelling to any other places, an officer is eligible to get only the train fare of 2nd Tier AC Compartment.***

*Arindam :- **Ok! Let me consult about it with my better half.***

****

*Runa (Arindam 's wife):- **Yes! Yes! Book the tickets for going to Andaman. In any case, going to Goa in the month of February is not a good decision at all. December month is the best month to enjoy Goa.***

*Arindam :- **Ok!***

****

Location: Behala Zonal Office, Allahabad Bank

*Sumon :- **Arindam is going for a tour to Andaman. Here are his duly filled up LFC application forms.***

*Somnath(Senior Manager of Administration Department of Behala Zone):- **Baah! Tell him, that his LFC Tour will get sanctioned soon. Andaman is a nice place. We are planning to have our Guest House or Holiday Home at Port Blair very soon.***

Sumon :- ***Ok!***

****

Location: Kunchuberia Branch, Allahabad Bank

Sumon :- ***Your LFC Tour Sanction letter has come. So, you are taking Privilege Leave from 15th February 2016 to 20th February 2016. Enjoy the Andaman Tour. Have a happy and safe journey.***

Arindam :- ***Thank you.***

****

Location: Netaji Subhashchandra Bose International Airport Terminal 2, Kolkata

Driver of Ola Cab:- ***Sir, please take out the luggage quickly from the back side of the cab. I have to get out of this Terminal 2 area within 5 minutes; else the Airport Authority will charge the Parking fee on this cab. From Thakurpukur to Dumdum Airport, the meter billing shows 517 rupees.***

Arindam :- ***Take these 520 rupees. What about the printed bill?***

Driver of Ola Cab:- ***The soft copy of this invoice will be sent to your registered e-mail id and an SMS to your registered mobile number.***

****

Location: In front of Spicejet Counter inside Netaji Subhashchandra Bose International Airport Terminal 2, Kolkata

Computer Operator of Spicejet Counter:- ***Sir, the weight of your luggage is below 30 Kilograms(15X2 = 30 Kgs). Madam, the weight***

of your handbag is below 7 Kilograms. So, you can keep this handbag with you. Take the boarding passes and proceed for security check.

****

Location: Security Check Gate inside Netaji Subhashchandra Bose International Airport Terminal 2, Kolkata

A Security Guard:- ***Sir, please put your mobile handset and wallet in this tray. The tray will be passed through the scanning machine.***

Arindam :- ***Ok!***

****

Location: In front of Gate 22 inside Netaji Subhashchandra Bose International Airport Terminal 2, Kolkata

Arindam :- ***This new terminal of Dumdum Airport has a very modernized look.***

Runa :- ***Hmm, there are lots of shops inside this terminal also. These shops are selling European shoes, Italian books, Dark chocolates and look at that corner. That's a coffee corner where people can have some adda while having a cup of coffee.***

Arindam :- ***But, everything is too costly inside the airport.***

Runa :- ***By the way, how is Spicejet? Are the tickets too costly?***

Arindam :- ***No! Not at all! Spicejet and Indigo are more or less of same category. For going to Port Blair and coming back to Kolkata by flight, the total price of flight fares of Spicejet airlines in economy class for two persons is Rs. 29,600/-. Therefore, ticket fare per person for travelling 1307 Kilometres from Kolkata to Port Blair*** *or vice-versa is Rs. 7,400/-. Not too expensive! But, I don't have any idea about the services provided by Spicejet. I have travelled in Indian Airlines and Indigo Airlines. As a low cost flight, services of Indigo Airlines are quite satisfactory.*

Runa :- Ok! Ok! Now, the check-in for boarding at SG251 Airlines has started.

****

Location: Inside SG251 Spicejet flight

Pilot inside the cabin:- Passengers! Welcome to Spicejet. I hope that all our air-hosts and air-hostesses are taking good care of you. Please tighten up your seat belts and co-operate with our staffs. We will reach Port Blair after 2 hours 10 minutes. Enjoy the journey. Thanks for choosing Spicejet. Thank you!

****

Runa :- There is a male host in this flight. Strange!

Arindam :- There is nothing strange in it. Why should girls have all the fun! Is it a taboo for a man to become an air-host?

Runa :- Oh! Ha ha ha. Anyway, change the topic. Now, it is 12.10 PM. We will reach Port Blair at around 2.20 PM or so.

****

Arindam :- Foods in Spicejet is quite good. Look at their meal packet. A Bun, A sweet, A small pack of Amul Butter, Jeera Rice, Dal Makhani and Smoky Chicken Curry! Very delicious! Really, the tagline of Spicejet; 'Red, Hot, Spicy' suits their services. In any business, there are two services; one is 'Core Services' and another one is 'Extra Services'. Spicejet also gives some importance to those

'Extra Services' unlike other airlines company. As a net result, I can't say whether their brand value has increased or not, but, certainly it is one of the reasons for Spicejet to do profits in consecutive quarters and that too when the aviation industry is passing through a very tough business phase.

Runa :- ***Is Ajay Singh trying to become the 2nd Captain Gopinath?***

Arindam :- ***No idea, dear!***

An Air Hostess:- ***Excuse me! Sir! What beverages do you like to have?***

Arindam :- ***Oh! Ki goh? Ki cold drinks nebe?***

Runa :- ***Any orange flavoured cold drinks.***

An Air Hostess:- ***We have 'Mirinda' Cans.***

Runa :- ***No problem!***

Arindam :- ***Tahole, duto Mirinda Cans ee diye deen.***

An Air Hostess:- ***Ok! Sir!***

****

Pilot inside the cabin:- ***Passengers! We are about to land at Port Blair Airport within 10 minutes. Please fasten up your seat belts. There are so many airlines, but, still, you have chosen Spicejet Airlines. Thanks for choosing Spicejet Airlines. We hope to see you again in our flights. We also hope that you will recommend about Spicejet to your family members, relatives and friends. Thank you.***

****

Location: Outside Veer Savarkar International Airport, Port Blair

A Tamil Driver:- ***Which hotel, Sir?***

Arindam :- ***Palm Grove Eco Resort.***

A Tamil Driver:- ***Get in my cab, Sir. 150 rupees!***

Arindam :- ***Ok!***

****

Location: Inside Palm Grove Eco Resort

Receptionist:- ***This is your room key, Sir!***

Arindam :- ***Ok!***

****

Runa :- ***The campus of this resort is really good. There is a pond. There are hens and ducks. Lots of coconut and betel-nut trees. Rooms are of two types. Either it is Andamani Cottage or Nicobari Hut. Lovely ecological campus, I must say. See, I have spotted a squirrel and a cat.***

Arindam :- ***Aha! Let me click some photos of Andamani Cat and Squirrel.***

Runa :- ***Where will we go in the evening?***

Arindam :- ***To Cellular Jail to watch its Light and Sound Show in Hindi.***

****

Location: Brichgunj Chowk , Port Blair

Arindam :- ***We want to go to Cellular Jail. How much?***

Auto-rickshaw driver:- ***120 rupees, Sir!***

****

Location: Inside Auto-rickshaw

Arindam :- ***See, this auto-rickshaw is going through a road which is adjacent to Port Blair Airport. I can see a helipad also. Oh! That's the headquarter building of Indian Air Force. Actually, Veer Savarkar International Airport is in the middle of Port Blair and the main circular road circles around it.***

Runa :- ***Hmm.***

Auto-rickshaw driver:- ***Saab! Cellular Jail aa gaya hain. There is a separate queue for ladies too in front of the ticket counter.***

Arindam :- ***Ok! Take these 120 rupees.***

****

Location: In front of ticket counter of Cellular Jail

A Clerk inside the counter of Cellular Jail:- ***All sitting tickets for Hindi Light and Sound Show are booked. It will start at 5.30 PM. I have tickets for English Light and Sound Show which will start at 6.45 PM. The tickets for English Light and Sound show will be given from 5.45 PM onwards.***

Runa :- ***Jaah! We are late to reach here. It is already 5.15 PM.***

*Arindam :- **Ok! We will see the English version. No problem. At around 5.45 PM, we will come here to take the tickets for English version show only. Come on; let us sit at that patriotic park which is just at the opposite side of Cellular Jail. I can see so many statues of freedom fighters in this park. Let us sit in that park for a while.***

*Runa :- **Ok.***

****

*Location: **Patriotic Park at the opposite side of the main gate of Cellular Jail***

*A person inside that Park:- **Sir, you want to see Hindi version of Light and Sound Show?***

*Arindam :- **Yes! Of course!***

*A person inside that Park:- **Just after 5 minutes, they will start giving the Standing tickets for Hindi version of Light and Sound Show. Chair nahi milega toh kya hua, kahi pe bhi baith ke dekh lijiye show. Bahut saara baithne ka jagaah hain, jaise ki pipal perh ke neeche. Hindi wala show ee accha laagega aap ko. Just go and buy the tickets.***

*Arindam :- **Ok! Ok!***

****

*Location: **In front of a food stall near Medical Bus Stand, Port Blair.***

*Runa :- **I really liked that Light and Sound show. It was awesome. British people created a very strict jail in Andaman Island, because this island was cut-off from any other mainland. So in those days, even if a prisoner managed to get out of the jail, he had to survive in jungle like a tribal people or may get killed by tribal people of***

Andaman Island. That watch tower is in the central position of Cellular Jail. To go to any barrack from other barrack, you have to pass through the Central Tower Gate. So many freedom fighters were sent here to get the punishment of 'Saaja-e-Kaala paani.' Mahavir Singh, Butukeswar Dutt, Masterda Surya Sen, Veer Savarkar and many other brave freedom fighters had to suffer so much pain and cruelty inside this Cellular Jail.

Arindam :- ***On every occasion of hanging, three freedom fighters were hanged simultaneously and before hanging them, a siren sound was made to let the other prisoners know that three prisoners of this Cellular Jail will be hanged up today. Their dead body was tied with stones and buried under the sea water of Bay of Bengal. The privacy was so well maintained inside this jail that even the brothers of Veer Savarkar never got the information that Veer Savarkar is also in the same jail. Even Sher Ali Afridi, the freedom fighter who killed British General Mayo was also in this Cellular Jail. I really feel pity on that old pipal tree which witnessed the brutal history inside the Cellular Jail while standing at the same position for years after years. Though, so many hunger strikes by prisoners helped to break the British icebergs of cruelty after so much strong collisions from all ends. We are lucky enough to sit under that great old pipal tree inside the Cellular Jail.***

Runa :- ***There is a fire of freedom inside the Cellular Jail in remembrance of all the freedom fighters of Cellular Jail. After the British, the Japanese people came to Andaman to show their style of cruelty on the people of Andaman. The Japanese bunkers in Andaman Island remains as a historical symbol of 2nd World War. Though, side by side, it is also true that Netaji Subhashchandra Bose was the first Indian freedom fighter to raise the Indian Flag in Cellular Jail and declared about an autonomous parallel Indian Government in Andaman.***

Arindam :- ***There were 7 barracks in Cellular Jail attached with the Central Tower. Why it is only 3 barracks now?***

Runa :- The other 4 barracks have been used for constructing the Government Hospital. The name of this Government Hospital is G.B.Pant Hospital named after a renowned freedom fighter, Govind Ballabh Pant. This Bus Stand is named after that Government Medical Hospital only. That's why; the name of this Bus Stand is Medical Bus Stand. You finish this piece of pan fried momo. I am done with it.

Arindam :- Ok! This pan fried momo is really good. One plate costs only Rs. 50/- and consists of 6 pieces of pan fried momo. From here, we will go to Aberdeen Bazaar by Auto-Rickshaw.

Episode: - 02

Auto-Rickshaw Driver:- ***Sir, this is Aberdeen market.***

Arindam :- ***yeh lo 20 rupiya.***

****

Location: ***Aberdeen Market, Port Blair***

Arindam :- ***So, this is Aberdeen market. Oh! That is Mohanpura Bus Stand. Government buses of all routes of Port Blair start from here.***

Runa :- ***In the Light and Sound Show of Cellular Jail, the voice of the old pipal tree mentioned about the Battle of Aberdeen. A battle must have taken place at this place.***

Arindam :- ***Yes! You are right. Generally, Andaman was a dense forest island where wild animals such as leopards, elephants, monkeys, chimpanzees, etc used to reside. In those ancient days, Negro people of Africa continent were used as slaves by the White people all around the world. There is a myth that some Negro people ran away from the place of their White masters and made this island as their hiding place. Many historians are also of the opinion that African pirates used to hide their ships, looted treasures and themselves in this forest island. So, briefly, the tribal people or local inhabitants of Andaman Islands are of African origin. When British people constructed the Cellular Jail and kept several Indian prisoners inside the Jail, the tribal people of Andaman Island felt insecure and were scared of their survival in future. Hence, as usual, the battle between tribal people of Andaman and British Armies took place at Aberdeen. Had those tribal people won that battle, maybe, Andaman would have not developed into a tourist destination.***

Runa :- ***In the Light and Sound show, it was mentioned that the name 'Andaman' came from the name of Bajrangbali.***

Arindam :- **Quite true. During Chola Empire in South India, several naval expeditions took place towards South-east Asian nations and at that time, Andaman Islands were used as a naval dock or base-station to get some refreshment while going for a long sea tour towards South-East Asia. So, gradually, in that process, lots of Hindus of South India started settling in these Islands. Many Hindus among them were devotee of Bhagwan Ram and Bhagwan Bajrangbali. In Tamil language, Hanuman is known as 'Anuman'. In South-Eastern Malay language, Hanuman is known as 'Andoman'. So, somehow, fusion of Hanuman's name in two languages got a new name, 'Andaman', which is the name of this island. Wait, let me buy some bananas. Like Kerala, in Andaman also, the quality of bananas and coconuts are very good too. How much 1 dozen of bananas cost?**

A Bangladeshi Muslim shopkeeper of fruits stall:- **Dada, ekhane kilo dar e bikri hoy, dozen e noy?**

Arindam :- **Accha! Accha! Thik ache! 4 te kala daao. Kato?**

A Bangladeshi Muslim shopkeeper of fruits stall:- **20 rupees only.**

Arindam :- **Ok! Take these 20 rupees. Koi go, chalo Aberdeen market er bhetorh taa dekhe asi kamon?**

****

Runa :- **There are so many bakery and jewel shops in this Aberdeen market. Generally, Tamil people have a soft corner towards golden jewels. Cakes in these bakery shops are of good quality too.**

Arindam :- **This Aberdeen market somewhat looks like a mini Anna Nagar market of Chennai. Oi dekho, kato baro baro nakul daana.**

This shop has so many items which are solely used during any puja of any Hindu God or Goddess. Aberdeen market is surely a standard market area of Port Blair. State Bank of India is having a big branch just at the opposite side of Mohanpura Bus Stand. We will walk a little distance to reach that four-lane crossing where Allahabad Bank is having its own branch. We will board a local bus from there to reach Brichgunj Chowk.

Runa :- ***Ok! No problem! But, buy 1 half-litre Fanta cold drinks please.***

Arindam :- ***Ok!***

****

Location: ***Palm Grove Eco Resort***

Arindam :- ***We want to go to Wandoor Beach and then to Jolly Buoy Island.***

Receptionist:- ***No, Sir! To go to Jolly Buoy Island, you have to apply for a permit 1 day before the day of visit. If you go today to Wandoor, you will not get the permit to go to Jolly Buoy Island.***

Arindam :- ***Are the corals of Jolly Buoy Island too good?***

Receptionist:- ***Sir! There are three points in Andaman, where corals are very popular. North Bay Island, Jolly Buoy Island and Neil Island! For Sea Walk, the best place is Havelock Island. If you want to see the best corals of Andaman, visit North Bay Island.***

Arindam :- ***Ok! Then! We will go to Wandoor beach only. Book a car please.***

Receptionist:- ***Ok! Sir! Andaman Eco Tours and Travels is always ready to serve you. The Tata Sumo will start from here at 10 AM***

tomorrow. You have to give Rs. 1000/- for going to Wandoor Beach and coming back to the resort after spending around 4 or 5 hours in Wandoor.

Arindam :- ***Ok.***

****

Location: ***Inside Tata Sumo Car***

Arindam :- ***How far is Wandoor from here?***

Tamil Hindu Driver:- ***Around 20 Kilometres, Sir!***

Arindam :- ***Ok! Oi dekho Bharat Sevashram Sangh er Holiday Home! Actually, this Garacharma and Buthu Basthi are developed areas in the outskirts of Port Blair. Garacharma means the skin of White people. Buthu Basthi means the colonies of tribal people. Hence, we may come to the conclusion that the British people created their own colonies just beside the colonies of Jarawa tribes of South Andaman in this region. Point to be noted here that uncivilized Jarawas does not exist in South Andaman. Maybe, some Jarawas have become civilized and they got mixed with the civilized society of South Andaman.***

Runa :- ***Then, where are the real uncivilized Jarawas of Andaman?***

Arindam :- ***That I don't know. Yeh, Jarawa log kahan dikhne ko milega?***

Tamil Hindu Driver:- ***In Baratang area of North and Middle Andaman. Saab! Yeh Marine Museum hain Wandoor ka. Just visit this Museum for half an hour. After that, we will go towards Wandoor Beach.***

Arindam :- ***Ok.***

****

Location: Inside Marine Museum of Wandoor

Runa :- See! This is the statue of a sea species known as Dugong.

Arindam :- Babah! I am hearing this name for the first time. It looks neither like a Sea Lion nor like a dolphin!

Runa :- It is known as Sea Cow as it is a herbivorous mammal. This species is on the verge of extinction.

Arindam :- Oh! Statue of a big crocodile inside the museum! Some beaches of Andaman Islands are the hunting hubs of crocodiles. In many beaches in Andaman, you will see a common signboard, 'Beware of Crocodiles'. There is also a statue of Sea Turtle. Basically, Andaman Islands are the best places for Sea Turtles to lay their eggs. Every year, several Sea Turtles come to Andaman beaches to lay their eggs.

Runa :- Why not! After all; Andaman waters are one of the safest zones for aquatic animals because fishing is not allowed in the waters nearer to the good beaches of Andaman Islands. Fishermen of Andaman Islands venture into the far away areas of Bay of Bengal to do fishing. That's why; fishes residing near the coastal areas of Andaman Islands have a very peaceful life and live for many years.

Arindam :- What's that inside the big glass-box? Wow! Replicas of all corals are kept inside this glass-box. There are buttons outside the glass-box with names of corals written beside each button. You press a button, the small white light glows inside the glass-box to show you the respective coral. Good one!

A staff of Marine Museum of Wandoor:- ***Sir, please proceed to our auditorium to watch a small film on the aquatic life of Wandoor beach.***

****

Location: ***Inside Tata Sumo Car***

Tamil Hindu Driver:- ***Sir! Woh aquatic animals wala video kaisa laaga?***

Arindam :- ***Accha hee hain! I was amazed to see Zebra fish and Needle fish in that video. These two types of fishes are there in the waters of Andaman Islands!***

Tamil Hindu Driver:- ***Sir! There lies an entirely new surprising world under the sea waters surrounding Andaman Islands. If you get a chance, please go for scuba diving or sea walk. You will really enjoy the colourful world under the sea. Lijiye saab! Aa gaya Wandoor Beach. I will be here inside this car at this parking lot.***

Arindam :- ***Ok.***

****

Location: ***Wandoor Beach***

Arindam :- ***Daab khaabe? Daarao jiggesh kori. Daab kato kore goh?***

A Bengali Hindu Coconut seller:- ***20 taaka kore. 2 to debo?***

Arindam :- ***Diye daao.***

****

Runa :- ***The coconuts of this area are slightly reddish in colour and are bigger in size. Each big coconut contains around 1 litre of coconut water. Getting 1 litre of coconut water in just 20 rupees is far better than buying any cold drink.***

Arindam :- ***Yeah! Right! Eh! It's too hot in this region in this month of February only. This beach is so clean and waters are so crystal clear. Look there! A big tree got uprooted and a wooden guest house has been devastated. But! How?***

A Bengali Jhinuk-seller in Wandoor Beach:- ***Dada! 2 saptaho aagey jharh hoyechilo ei beach e teh, taate ei baro gaach uprey gache aar oi baari taah toh tachnach hoye gache. Those people are repairing that house.***

Arindam :- ***Oh! Accha! We can see a portion in the beach which has been encircled with a fence of nets and people are bathing within that encircled area only. Are there any reasons behind it?***

A Bengali Jhinuk-seller in Wandoor Beach:- ***Last month, a crocodile was spotted in the bushes of Wandoor Beach. That's why; the Tourism Department of Andaman Government took some security measures. Don't go near those bushes. Bushes are the ideal place for crocodiles to hide.***

Arindam :- ***Ok!***

Runa :- ***Time to have some photo sessions, dear. I am feeling thirsty after walking on this beach. Come on; let us go to that local shop to buy a bottle of cold drink.***

****

Location: ***Inside a local shop of Wandoor Beach***

*Arindam :- **Se ki! Printed price of half litre Fanta cold drinks is Rs. 34/- and you are taking Rs. 40/- from me.***

*Bengali Hindu shopkeeper:- **Dada! Aapni bangaali bole 40 taaka nilaam, foreigner der kaach theke toh amra 60 taaka nei. Tourist spot dada! Ekmatro tourist ele tobeyi amader sale hoy. Local people hardly buy cold drinks. They drink coconut waters only.***

*Runa :- **Are these marbles or stones kept inside a tray?***

*Bengali Hindu shopkeeper:- **Naa didimoni! These are actually the eggs of a local bird of Andaman Islands. These eggs are so well designed and small shaped by nature that it looks like designed marbles. Would you like to have omelette of these eggs?***

*Runa :- **Na na! Dorkaar nei. Koi goh, come on; let us walk towards the helipad of Indian Navy in Wandoor Beach.***

****

*Location: **Helipad of Indian Navy in Wandoor***

*Arindam :- **When the helicopter comes nearer to the helipad, it really creates an artificial wind storm indeed.***

*Runa :- **Let me click the photo of this navy blue coloured helicopter. I am feeling hungry now. There is no Bengali restaurant in the beachside of Wandoor.***

*Arindam :- **Let us sit back inside the Tata Sumo Car and if we find any Bengali restaurant during our journey, we will get down there and have our lunch.***

****

*Location: **Inside Tata Sumo Car***

Tamil Hindu Driver:- ***Sir! In front of the Marine Museum of Wandoor Beach, there is a Bengali restaurant. You can have your lunch there. Vegetarian thali is of Rs. 80/- only. Quite cheaper!***

Arindam :- ***Ok. After having lunch, on our way back towards Port Blair, we may visit Sippighat Farm.***

Tamil Hindu Driver:- ***Ok, Sir!***

****

Location: ***Sippighat Farm***

Arindam :- ***So many trees, so many flowers. There is a farmhouse too. Good place indeed. See, many people are giving waters to those trees. It is a well maintained farm.***

Runa :- ***Nothing so special. It is looking like any botanical garden only. But, yes, the quality of trees is really good. Credit goes to the maintenance staffs here. Time to go now! It is too hot out here during noon. Who will say that it is just the month of February?***

Arindam :- ***Geographically, Andaman Islands are parallel to Chennai. So, obviously, it's hot Andaman indeed. Come on, get inside the car. We will go to Cellular Jail again to visit it fully.***

****

Location: ***Inside Cellular Jail***

Arindam :- ***From the top of the watch tower, you can see both Ross Island and North Bay. Fantastic view indeed! Let us get down from here and visit the Cell of Veer Savarkar.***

Runa :- ***Wait, let me take a selfie with you here at the terrace of Cellular Jail.***

Arindam :- ***Those freedom fighters suffered so much cruelty inside this Cellular Jail to give freedom to Indians and we, Indians after getting freedom are taking our selfie photos inside the Cellular Jail. See the fun!***

Runa :- ***Had there been no freedom, could we have clicked our selfie photos? Taking selfie photos is also an act of freedom. We feel proud of those freedom fighters and we are proud to be Indians.***

Arindam :- ***Ha ha ha. Wise men in ancient days have rightly said that it is easy to fall in love with any woman but that much difficult to win war of words against any woman.***

Runa :- ***Accha! Ebaar nichey chalo. Already, the Security Guards are blowing whistles as a reminder to vacate the Cellular Jail before 5 PM as Lights and Sound show will start at 5.30 PM.***

Arindam :- ***There may be ghosts inside the Cellular Jail and they may come out at midnight to meet each other or have an adda session. So many prisoners have been executed in this jail. So, their souls are still roaming inside this Cellular Jail. We can create a story on Indian freedom struggle by making these ghosts as the lead characters in that story. Is it not a good idea?***

Runa :- ***Uff! You and your fantasy world! Come back to the real world, baby! See! This is the Cell where Veer Savarkar was kept.***

Arindam :- ***I will go inside a Cell of this Cellular Jail and you must take my photo. I am wearing an orange coloured T-Shirt too. In foreign nations, prisoners wear orange coloured uniform only.***

Runa :- ***But, every prisoner has a number inside a Jail. Hey! Prisoner! What is your Prisoner Number?***

Arindam :- ***999.***

Runa :- ***Ha ha ha.***

****

##

Episode – 03

Location: ***Outside Cellular Jail***

Arindam :- ***Where are these stairs leading to? See, just beside the Patriotic Park, there are staircases.***

Runa :- ***Let us go downwards by walking on these stairs. It is going towards Rajiv Gandhi Water Sports Complex Park. Come on.***

****

Location: ***Inside the premises of Rajiv Gandhi Water Sports Complex Park***

Arindam :- ***Baah! Lots of water sports take place here. Paddle boating, speed boating, etc. A portion of this water complex park has been encircled with big walls to create an enclosure of still waters where paddling boats can sail. All the other water sports like speed boating are on the sea waters only.***

Runa :- ***There is a jetty beside this Rajiv Gandhi Water Sports Complex Park. Ross Island is very nearer from this Jetty. In the ticket counter also, it is written that it costs Rs. 450/- per person to go to Ross Island and North Bay from here and return back at this Jetty again.***

Arindam :- ***This park is also a park for walking; it seems. I can see several local people of this area are walking from one end to the other. This place is suited for morning walks and evening walks. Aah! It's sunset time. The sky is having an orange coloured blend. Both of us are wearing orange coloured clothes too.***

Runa :- ***Wait, let me tell that guy to click our photo. Bhaiya! Please click our photo with our camera.***

A local boy:- ***Ok! Smile please! Now, stand at this side please by keeping the statue of Rajiv Gandhi as the background. Yeah! Completed!***

Arindam and Runa :- ***Thank you!***

A local boy:- ***Always welcome.***

Arindam :- ***Come on. Now, we will go to the Corbyn Cove Beach.***

****

Location: ***In front of food stalls inside a Bus Stand near Rajiv Gandhi Water complex Park***

Runa :- ***This Pau Bhaji is far better than chicken momo.***

Arindam :- ***Inside Chicken momo, sometimes, the meats are not roasted properly. But, in Pau Bhaji, there is no such risk. Local people of Andaman love to eat Pau Bhaji. Generally, 'Pau' word has become famous in India due to Mumbaikars. Hardly will you find any Mumbaikar who don't like to eat 'Vada Pau'.***

Runa :- ***It's already 5.40 PM now. Time to go to Corbyn Cove Beach!***

Arindam :- ***Yeah! Yeah! Auto! Yeh auto Corbyn Cove ko jaata? Kitna leta?***

Auto-Rickshaw Driver:- ***100 rupees, Sir!***

****

Location: ***Corbyn Cove Beach***

Runa :- ***What are these on this beach?***

Arindam :- Japanese bunkers. This Corbyn Cove beach is on the north-eastern side of South Andaman Island. The naval forces of Japan took control of these areas of Andaman Island.

Runa :- In this beach, the sea waters do make some noise. There are some sea waves here in this beach. People who are fans of Digha beach and Puri beach will surely like this Corbyn Cove Beach. There are lots of coconut trees on this beach. Ambience is perfect for married couples.

Arindam :- That's why; many tourists always prefer to book hotels nearer to Corbyn Cove Beach. But, where is the Snake Island? I have heard about Snake Island which is nearer to Corbyn Cove Beach.

Runa :- We should spend around 20 minutes here and then go back to our hotel. Tomorrow, we have to start our journey at 3.30 AM to go to Baratang Island.

Arindam :- Oh! Yes! It was out of my mind that I booked for Baratang Tour package tomorrow for Rs. 3900/- and Havelock Tour package on day after tomorrow for Rs. 5300/-. Chalo, chalo, hotel e firey jaai. Kheye deye taratari suye porte hobe je.

****

Location: Palm Grove Eco Resort

Arindam :- Gaadi aa gaya hain kya?

Sathya (Manager of Palm Grove Eco Resort):- Yes, Sir!

Arindam :- I am still yawning, you see! It's only 3.25 AM.

Sathya:- Ha ha ha. Sir! Baratang is too far away from here and there are several restrictions in that area. Earlier you go and earlier you come back is safer. See there! The entire tour party under

Captain Nilesh is getting ready to get into that small bus which is also going to Baratang. All the tourists under Captain Nilesh are wearing a white coloured cap where the name of 'Captain Nilesh' is printed. The Tata Sumo is standing there, Sir! You can get inside the car. It is 3.30 AM now.

Arindam :- ***Ok.***

****

Location: ***Inside the Tata Sumo Car***

Arindam :- ***Baratang bahut dur hain kya?***

Nepali Driver:- ***Jee saab! 100 kilometres from here! At around 5 AM, we will reach the Ferrargunj Checkpost. Both of you have taken your Voter ID card with you, naah!***

Arindam :- ***Yeah! Yeah!***

Nepali Driver:- ***Fill up these two permit forms, Sir! Your name, father's name, address, mobile number and Voter ID number! Also provide the name of your spouse, father name of your spouse, paternal address of your spouse, mobile number of your spouse and voter ID number of your spouse. Another permit application form will be given to me by the officials of Ferrargunj Checkpost. You have to fill up that form also. Please fill up these two permit forms.***

Arindam :- ***Ki goh, tomar Voter ID Card taa daao, Voter ID number taa likhe niyi form e.***

Runa :- ***Ei naao. Don't you think we are going through the same road that goes to Wandoor.***

Arindam :- ***Hmm, taai toh mone hocche. Accha! Yeh gaadi Wandoor ho ke jaayega kya?***

Nepali Driver:- ***Nahi saab! We are going through Great Andaman Trunk Road. Just after sometime, you will see a road going towards left side. That road leads to Wandoor. We will go through Great Andaman Trunk Road only passing by Tusnabad area to reach Ferrargunj Checkpost. Point to be noted here that 4 convoys are allowed per day to pass through Ferrargunj Checkpost. Each convoy may have 30 vehicles at maximum. A military jeep with commandos will lead each convoy and one local police jeep will be at the end of the convoy. These security measures are being taken to keep the tourists safe from any attacks from the people of Jarawa tribe. Photography is not allowed while going through the areas of Jarawa tribe. Any car of the convoy is not allowed to stand anywhere in between. Tourists are not allowed to give any food to any person of Jarawa tribe. If any of these rules and regulations gets violated then a tourist may get a penalty of Rs. 10,000/- or 3 years to 7 years of imprisonment. Even the driver or guide will not be spared. They will also face some punishment.***

Arindam :- ***The administration of Andaman is very strict indeed!***

Nepali Driver:- ***Pehle nahi tha, abhi Andaman Government ko strict hona pada. Few years back, some people of Jarawa tribe died after eating outside foods given to them by the foreign tourists. In one instance, the video footage of Jarawa people dancing in front of camera became a shameful thing for Andaman Administration. Many a times, Jarawa people have attacked the tourists. That's why; Andaman Government is so strict nowadays. Now, the Andaman Government provide foods to Jarawa people. Lijiye saab! Aa gaya Ferrargunj Checkpost. Give me the duly filled up permit forms. Let me submit it to the Checkpost office. In the meantime, you can have your breakfast here. The cars will pass through checkpost at 6 AM. Now, it is only 4.55 AM. Just beyond that checkpost, there is a Sulabh Complex. You can freshen up there. You may visit a tribal temple near the checkpost also. Have your***

breakfast now. I will be back within 10 minutes with another form that you have to fill up.

Arindam :- ***Ok!***

****

Location: ***In front of a food stall just at half a metre distance from Ferrargunj Checkpost***

Runa :- ***Idli tastes good, but not the sambhar and coconut chatni.***

Arindam :- ***Yes, I agree with you. I think that it is too much to expect that Andamani people will cook South Indian curries like South Indians do.***

****

Location: ***In front of Ferrargunj Police Chowki***

Arindam :- ***This is an awesome forest area. Behind that Police Station, is the hilly forest. Just at the opposite side of the Police Station, there is a farmland, a house with a hilly forest background. The Sunrise in the sky beyond that hilly forest making it look more beautiful!***

Runa :- ***It is around 5.45 AM now. Come on, let us visit that tribal temple and go back to our car.***

Arindam :- ***Several Government buses go to Diglipur, Kadamtala, Rangat and Maya Bandar. All those buses have to pass through this checkpost only after proper verifications.***

****

Location: ***Inside Tata Sumo Car***

Nepali Driver:- ***O dekhiye saab, ek Jarawa on the left side of this road.***

Runa :- ***Wow! A Jarawa woman making a basket while sitting in front of her hut!***

Arindam :- ***That Jarawa woman looks like a Black African woman and was wearing only some leaves to cover only the sensitive portions of her body.***

Nepali Driver:- ***Sir! They are trying hard to become civilized. But, there is a conservative group among Jarawa people who neither wants to get civilized nor allows any other Jarawa people to maintain any link with any civilized people. That's the real problem! Mentality of Jarawa people are still in the Stone Age! They are still so uncivilized!***

Arindam :- ***Why blame Jarawas only? I can show you several civilized people in this world whose mentality is also in the Stone Age.***

Nepali Driver:- ***Look there, Sir! On the right side of the road, some Jarawa children are playing with bows and arrows.***

Runa :- ***Oi dekho! That Jarawa boy threw a small pebble towards our window.***

Nepali Driver:- ***Window ka glass utha ke rakhiye, Sir! Jarawa people are wild enough to throw pebbles towards the car.***

Arindam :- ***Ok! These Jarawa children were totally naked. So, obviously, these Jarawa children are more uncivilized than that Jarawa woman.***

Runa :- ***Ha ha ha. Khub majaa peyecho dekhchi! Have you watched the Bengali film, 'Sabuj Dwiper Raja'?***

Arindam :- ***Of course! I have seen that movie. The story was based on Andaman Island.***

****

Nepali Driver:- ***Saab! We have reached Middle Strait Jetty. From here, you have to board the Ferry boat to reach Oralkatcha Jetty of Baratang Island. The Ferry boat will take Rs. 7/- per person. From Oralkatcha Jetty, a speed boat will take you towards the Baratang Limestone Cave. That speed boat ticket is Rs. 450/- per person! Give me Rs. 900, Sir! Main ticket booking kar doonga jaldi se. You don't have to stand in a long queue after reaching Baratang Jetty.***

Arindam :- ***Ok! Take these 900 rupees.***

****

Location: *On the Ferry Vessel*

Arindam :- ***This ferry vessel also ferry four-wheelers, trucks and buses. This ferry vessel is almost similar to the ferry vessel which is used in Hatania Duania River of Namkhana. Though, this ferry vessel is somewhat bigger in size.***

Runa :- ***It takes around 20 minutes by ferry vessel to reach Oralkatcha Jetty (Baratang Island Jetty) from Middle Strait Jetty.***

****

Location: *Baratang Island Jetty*

A tourist from Delhi:- ***I am feeling scared! Is it too risky to have a ride on the speedboat? Crocodiles are there in this water. Even***

those islands at both sides of the sea water are dense forests only. Jarawas can attack us with bows and arrows!

A staff of Baratang Island Jetty:- ***Nothing will happen. Just relax! I am working in this area for 15 years. Till date, no such casualties have taken place in this place. Wear the life jacket and remember the name of your speedboat. After reaching the core area of Baratang Island, we will leave you to the island to have a visit to the Limestone cave. After seeing the Limestone cave, you have to come back to the Jetty ghat of that forest area. We will call the passenger by speedboat name only. The name of your speedboat is Ganga-II.***

****

Location: In Ganga-II speedboat

Runa :- ***It is really an amazing experience to go through two islands with such a speed. Moreover, we are travelling on the waters of Bay of Bengal.***

Arindam :- ***The topography of this island is quite similar to Sunderbans delta. There are lots of Sundri or mangrove trees out here. We are now entering through the forest of mangrove trees to reach the jetty area of the core area of Baratang Island.***

A tourist from Gurgaon:- ***Mast adventure hain yaar! It is reminding me of a scene in 'Anaconda' film. Kaash yeh Amazon River hota!***

Wife of that tourist from Gurgaon:- ***Toh phir hum dono Anaconda ke pet mein jaake honeymoon manaate. Mast adventure hota nahi?***

Everyone in that speedboat (laughed heartily):- ***Ha ha ha...***

Lifeboy of Speedboat:- ***We have reached the core area. But, please remain seated till we tell you to stand up. The speedboat generally topples in shallow waters, not in deep waters.***

Sailor of Speedboat:- ***Anchor the speedboat. Ok! Now, all of you can stand up and leave the boat to have a visit to the core area. But, no outside food packets are allowed. You are only allowed to take a bottle of water with you.***

****

###

Episode – 04

Location: Core area of Baratang Island

Arindam :- ***This must be a tribal village area. There are so many birds in this island. This road is a cliffy one. Too many ups and downs on our way! Be careful! These stony stairs are slippery.***

Runa :- ***Aah! After a long walk, there is a place where local people of this island are selling cucumbers and lemon water. But, we will drink it after coming back from the Limestone Cave which is just at a few metres distance from here.***

****

Location: Inside Baratang Limestone Cave

A guide of Baratang Island:- ***During rainy season, we can see several drops of water falling from that sink hole which is at that upward portion of this cave. This is such a limestone cave, where***

Mother Nature has created lots of beautiful architectures with the help of water and wind. Look at this portion of this cave. It is a natural idol of Bhagwan Ganesh. Look there! The limestone lotus facing the earth! Look at this portion. It is the tiger's claw. Come to this place, please. Here, the limestone takes the golden colour.

Arindam :- ***Baah! Daarun! Prakriti r yeh ak aparup srishti. Chokhe naa dekhle biswas ee koraa jaayena.***

Runa :- ***It is too hot ,dark and stuffy inside. Let us now go out of this cave. I am feeling thirsty.***

****

Location: In front of a Neebu Paani Stall at a village area of Baratang Island

Runa :- ***Aah! This Neebu Paani refreshed my body.***

Arindam :- ***Yeah! Of course! Actually, we came to this spot by taking a long and difficult route. If you go diagonally through this farming land, you will easily reach the Jetty area within a short time. Bhai! Hum log ish zameen se paidal jaa sakte hain kya?***

Owner of Lemon Water Stall:- ***No! Sir! Tourists are not allowed to enter any field of any tribal people of this Island; otherwise, the tribal people may attack you. You have to walk by that route only which has been authorized only for tourists.***

A local blackish coloured dog of that island (hungry for food):- ***Hae! Hae!***

Runa :- ***Ehe! This dog is sitting near me and trying to bite on my handbag. He is so hungry, I hope!***

Arindam :- ***Ha ha ha...daarao er saathe ektu majaa kori. Ki re kaalu, khidey peyeche? Kono khabaar nei amader kache. Jaa khabaar chilo sab boat e rekhe esechi. Taa haan re, toder ei island e mangsho hoy? Mangsho khetey paash?***

A local blackish coloured dog of that island (barked with emotions out of anger and frustration and went away from there):- ***Ghuuu! Ghuuu! Ghu! Oooh!***

Arindam :- ***Bye! Bye! Kaalu!***

Runa :- ***Dhaath! It is a dog! What will it understand?***

Arindam :- ***Animals understand everything but they can't express anything in words. Maybe, that's why; humans are termed as the only social animal of this planet, though literally. Actually, so called unsocial animals of jungle are more social than so called social animals of the world.***

Runa :- ***Everything is going above my head. Come on; let us go back to the Jetty area.***

****

Location: ***Jetty area in core area of Baratang Island***

Arindam :- ***Please click a photo of me. I am standing by holding a trunk of a mangrove tree.***

Runa :- ***You are behaving like a junglee person now. Why jungle always attracts you, I really don't know. Thik kore daarao, arek baar chobi tuli. Aager baarey amaar haath kenpey gache.***

Lifeboy of Ganga –II Speedboat:- ***Passengers of Ganga-II speedboat, please get inside the speedboat.***

*Arindam :- **Ei chalo, chalo, amader majhi bhai amaader daakche.***

****

*Location: **Baratang Island Jetty***

*Nepali Driver:- **Sir, would you like to go to the Mud Island? It will cost only Rs. 500/-. Half an hour journey from here! There is an active mud volcano on that island. Some pirates also live in that island as per unofficial records. Jaayenge Sir?***

*Arindam :- **Ki goh? Jaabe naaki?***

*Runa :- **To see a mud volcano! Naah! Jaabo naa. Nahi jayenge humlog.***

*Nepali Driver:- **Ok! Next ferry vessel is at 12.05 PM. Now, it is 11.35 AM. Aap log restroom mein baithiye. Yeh ferry vessel se ush paar chale jaayenge. From Middle Strait Jetty, we will start at 12.30 PM as that is the time for the 1st convoy to go out of Jarawa Reserve Checkpost.***

*Arindam :- **Ok! Ei coolfi malai khaabe? A man is selling coolfi malai for Rs. 20/-. Wait; let me buy two coolfi malai.***

****

*Location: **Jarawa Reserve Checkpost***

*Runa (while sitting inside Tata Sumo Car):- **See! Those military commandos! They are checking the car number and tallying with a document paper in their hands. Another commando is standing with a handycam and doing video recording of all the cars of 1st convoy that are going out of the Jarawa Reserve Checkpost.***

Arindam :- ***This area must be a buffer zone. This buffer zone is created by the Andaman Government to prevent the extinction of Jarawa tribal people.***

****

Location: ***Inside Tata Sumo Car***

Nepali Driver:- ***Sir! See, there are some Jarawa youngsters having an adda session on that culvert.***

Runa :- ***Wow! But, these Jarawa youngsters are well-dressed.***

Arindam :- ***Yeah, they are wearing shirts and pants. One Jarawa teenage boy was wearing a hat made of leaves. He was chewing betel leaf and his lips were too red. That teenage Jarawa boy gave a smile when I stared at him. His teeth were somewhat blackish. Anyway, some Jarawa youngsters are becoming modernized, it seems.***

Runa :- ***I am feeling too hungry now. When will we have our lunch?***

Nepali Driver:- ***Sir! There is a good South Indian hotel near Ferrargunj Checkpost. You can have lunch there only. I will also have lunch there only.***

****

Location: ***Ferrargunj Checkpost Area***

Arindam :- ***Baah! This South Indian meal is tasty. This is a real South Indian Restaurant. Oho! They have not given Rasham. Anna! Thoda Rasham dena ji.***

Runa :- ***Rasham! What's that?***

Arindam :- ***I don't know exactly, how Rasham is prepared! But, the combination of sour taste of tamarind and spicy taste of red chilli is really delicious.***

Runa :- ***I love Sambhar only and sour curd. But, it is strange to see that in this restaurant, there is no sour curd in the South Indian vegetable thali.***

****

Location: ***Inside the Dining Hall of Palm Grove Eco Resort***

Runa :- ***You order a Tomato Soup and I am ordering a Chicken noodle soup.***

Arindam :- ***Well, nothing can be better than that to spend the evening inside this Dining Hall. Tomorrow, we have to start our journey towards Havelock Island at 6.30 AM.***

****

Location: ***Palm Grove Eco Resort***

Receptionist:- ***Sir! Both of you are ready, naah! The Tata Sumo car driver is waiting outside. It is already 6.30 AM. Please ensure that both of you have taken your Voter ID Cards.***

Arindam :- ***Ok! Yeah! We have taken our Voter ID Cards with us.***

****

Location: ***Inside the Tata Sumo Car***

Arindam :- ***Are we going to Aberdeen Jetty?***

North Bihari Driver:- ***No, Sir! We are going to Phoenix Bay Jetty. At the gate of that Jetty, the security guards will check your tickets and respective Voter ID. Then from the ticket counter of that Jetty, you will get your respective boarding pass. Tickets ka price kitna liya Sir?***

Arindam :- ***For going to Havelock by MV Makruzz Catamaran ferry boat and returning back to Phoenix Bay Jetty, the ticket price per head is Rs. 1950/- per head.***

North Bihari Driver:- ***You booked the tickets through the hotel, right?***

Arindam :- ***Yeah!***

North Bihari Driver:- ***Actually, the ticket price is Rs. 1900/- per head. The Hotel management acted as an agent, that's why; they charged extra Rs. 50/- on each ticket. Anyway, agent hota hee hain commission lene ke liye. We will reach Phoenix Bay Jetty within 20 minutes.***

****

Location: **Phoenix Bay Jetty**

North Bihari Driver:- ***Sir, four-wheelers and two-wheelers are not allowed beyond this point for security reasons. You have to walk for a few minutes from here to reach the main gate of Phoenix Bay Jetty. Mera phone number le lijiye. When you return back from Havelock at around 5.30 PM, just give me a call if you fail to find this Tata Sumo Car at this place.***

Arindam :- ***Ok!***

****

*Location: **Passenger waiting room inside Phoenix Bay Jetty***

*Arindam :- **Actually, this Phoenix Bay Jetty is under Indian Navy. Some ships are getting repaired at that corner of this Jetty. Almost all the staffs are of Indian Navy.***

*Runa :- **Please go and collect the boarding pass by showing the printed copy of our tickets which has been booked online through Palm Grove Eco Resort.***

*Arindam :- **Haan jacchi.***

****

*Arindam :- **So many European girls are going to Havelock Island. See, all those tall ladies with big bags at their backside. They must be going for Scuba diving and Sea walks. These European girls and boys are so adventurous.***

*Runa :- **Don't give too much importance to them by staring at them. These European girls may think that Indian boys like you are too fond of European girls.***

*Arindam :- **Are you feeling uneasy because I am staring at them. Ha ha ha.***

*Runa :- **Ok! I will also stare at those European boys. Oho! See, that European boy is so handsome and looks like Sylvester Stallone.***

*Arindam :- **That European girl is looking like Kate Winslet, only this girl's hair is slightly too blackish.***

*Runa :- **Thamo! Onek earki holo. They are making some announcements.***

A Staff of Phoenix Bay Jetty:- ***All the passengers of MV Makruzz Catamaran ferry boat are requested to board the MV Makruzz Catamaran now. MV Makruzz Catamaran ferry boat will start its journey towards Havelock at 8.30 AM and reach Havelock at 10.35 AM.***

****

Location: ***Inside MV Makruzz Catamaran Ferry Boat***

Arindam :- ***This is a different type of a vessel indeed, though, fully air-conditioned.***

Runa :- ***Let me take some photos.***

Arindam :- ***Oh! Selfie! Ok!***

Runa :- ***An European man is sitting beside you. He belongs to which nation. Ask him?***

Arindam :- ***Hi! You are from which nation?***

A German tourist:- ***From Berlin City of Germany? You are from?***

Arindam :- ***India.***

A German tourist:- ***India is a very big nation. From which city of India?***

Arindam :- ***City of Joy!***

A German tourist:- ***Which is the City of Joy in India?***

Arindam :- ***Kolkata!***

A German tourist:- ***Sorry! Kolkata?***

Arindam :- ***Calcutta. I am from Calcutta.***

A German tourist:- ***Oh! Calcutta! British people created that city. I have heard that it is a good city. If possible, I may visit Calcutta once.***

Arindam :- ***Yeah! Sure!***

Runa :- ***You are expert in confusing any person. This man is going to Havelock with his father, mother and wife. His father's face is very rough and tough like Hitler.***

Arindam :- ***No! No! His father looks like Klinsman, the German footballer. The ferry boat has started its journey. The lifeboy inside this boat looks like a bouncer of any bar. Watch the video on that TV Screen. The video is about security purposes during emergency in this MV Makruzz. There are four emergency doors in this MV Makruzz. Life jackets are kept below the seat of each passenger. During extreme emergency, passengers are safely transferred to four life boats attached with this MV Makruzz. Good!***

Runa :- ***This journey is so smooth. Maybe, we are travelling downstream, that's why; it is such a smooth journey. Still around 40 minutes left to reach Havelock Island. Let me have a nap. You keep on watching the sponsored videos of CNN-IBN Channel regarding Havelock Island Tour.***

****

##

Episode – 05

*Location: **Havelock Island Jetty***

*Arindam :- **So, we are in Havelock Island now. This jetty is so clean and tidy! Let me click some photos here.***

*Runa :- **The cab will be waiting for us outside the jetty?***

*Arindam :- **Yes! A cab driver will be standing in front of the jetty with my name printed boldly on a white paper. Sathya, the manager of Palm Grove Eco Resort booked that car for us for Rs. 800/-. The Tata Sumo Car was booked for Rs. 600/-.***

****

Location: Outside Havelock Island Jetty

Arindam :- ***Chaliye! I am Arindam.***

Bengali Driver:- ***Cholun dada! Edike aasun. Ei Maruti Van e bosun. You are from Kolkata?***

Arindam :- ***Yes! Koi goh! Bosey paro gaarite. How far is Radhanagar Beach from here?***

Bengali Driver:- ***Around 14 Kilometres, Sir!***

****

Location: Inside Maruti Van

Arindam :- ***Beautiful Island! Shops are having Bengali names. There are so many temples of Bengali Gods and Goddesses. There are coconut trees in plenty. Even there are so many betelnut trees.***

Runa :- ***The soil of this island must be very fertile.***

Arindam :- ***Ekhaane bachor e katobaar chassh hoy?***

Bengali Driver:- ***Ekhane beshir bhaag jomi ee trifashali jomi. I mean, crops are grown for three times in a year on almost all the fertile fields of this island.***

****

Bengali Driver:- ***Sir, we have reached Radhanagar Beach. The beach is just a few metres from here. All the Bengali hotels are in this street only. You can have your breakfast at Sagarika Hotel as it is the best Bengali hotel among all the Bengali hotels here. Now, it is 11.25 AM. When is your departure time from Havelock Island Jetty?***

Arindam :- ***At 3.30 PM. We will be at this place again at around 2.15 PM.***

Bengali Driver:- ***Ok! Sir! No problem.***

****

Location: ***Sagarika Hotel at Radhanagar Beach***

Owner of Sagarika Hotel:- ***Ki khaben bolun? Idli na Parota?***

Arindam :- ***Parota ee din. We will get lunch in this hotel, naah?***

Owner of Sagarika Hotel:- ***Of course! Bengali meal is available. Sabji Bhaath meal 130 taaka!***

Arindam :- ***Quite expensive!***

Runa :- ***It has to be as it is a tourist spot.***

****

Location: ***Radhanagar Beach***

Arindam :- ***See! There is a gate where it is written, 'Welcome to Radhanagar Beach'. I can see a Police Control Room and a Lifeboy Control Room here in this beach. Beach administration is very strong out here.***

Runa :- ***So far, this is the best beach which we have seen in Andaman Islands. The sands are so crystal clear that even the clouds are getting its reflection on the sands. As if these sands are a natural mirror.***

Arindam :- ***Now, I understand why people spend at least 2 days in Havelock Island in their trip to Andaman Island. This Radhanagar Beach is a fabulous beach to enjoy bathing and swimming in the sea waters. Had we known about this Radhanagar Beach earlier, we could have booked a hotel in Havelock for 2 days.***

Runa :- ***To enjoy bathing in sea waters of Radhanagar Beach, you don't need to book a hotel in Havelock Island. There are changing rooms available for both gents and ladies. Even there are dresses on rent to swim in the sea water. If you want, you can easily enjoy bathing now only in Radhanagar Beach.***

Arindam :- ***Hmm...jaak ge baad daao. We will just walk on the sea beach bare-footed. I can see some white skinned men and women swimming there on this beach. They are foreigners.***

Runa :- ***Those girls are wearing bikinis. That's why; your eyes are going towards them. Really, men are men and will remain men.***

Arindam :- ***Aah! You are trying to make an issue about it, whereas nothing is so serious in it. Really, women are women and will remain women. Wait; let me tell that foreign guy to click a photo of ours. Please, if you can click a photo of ours.***

A white-skinned bulky man wearing a half pant (While walking on the beach with his girlfriend):- ***Sure! Why not! Both of you please stand closer. Both of you keep your one hand on each other's shoulder. Yeah! Nice one. The photo has been clicked.***

Arindam :- ***Thank you! Thank you very much.***

A white-skinned bulky man wearing a half pant:- ***Always welcome!***

Runa :- ***You are such a naughty boy! You intentionally requested that guy to click our photo, so that you can have some time to***

watch those girls in his group who were wearing bikinis and standing beside him.

Arindam :- ***Aah! In this desolate part of this beach, no other person is there to click our photo. That's why; I requested that guy. Where are your shoes?***

Runa :- ***Oho! I kept the shoes at that point of the beach. I forgot about the shoes while walking on this beach barefooted with you. Thank God! The water current of sea water has not taken away my shoes. Look there! I can see a small cruise and some speed boats.***

Arindam :- ***That is the cruise of these foreign tourists. They anchored the cruise at the deep waters and came to this Radhanagar Beach by the speed boats to enjoy bathing. These speed boats are kept attached with that cruise only. Can you spot that Yacht? That Yacht is also of foreign tourists. These foreign girls and boys who are tanning their skin here in Radhanagar Beach are the passengers of that Yacht only.***

Runa :- ***We are walking on this sea beach for half an hour. Let us go towards that forest area on the right side of the Radhangar Beach. There is a wooden watch tower which is broken at its front side. We will go and sit on the top of that watch tower. Come on.***

****

Location: On a wooden watch tower at Radhanagar Beach

Arindam :- ***Crocodiles may remain hidden in these bushes. What will you do if they come out from these jungle bushes?***

Runa :- ***Dhaath! Crocodiles don't have fear or what! Crocodiles are also scared of humans, especially on lands. This is such a lovely place. Clear sky on top, lovely ambience of a forest and a beautiful sea beach on front of us! I am feeling so romantic now. Oi***

bhadralok ke balo na, amader ekta chobi tuley debe. We are sitting on top of a broken watch tower. There should be a photo of it.

Arindam :- ***Excuse me, Sir! Can you please click a photo of us while we are sitting on top of this broken watch tower?***

A Gujarati Tourist:- ***Arrey! Kyon nahi! Give me the camera. Smile please! Here I go! Yeah! The photo has been clicked. Dekh lijiye, thikthak click hua hain toh?***

Arindam :- ***Yeah! Ekdum perfect!***

A Gujarati Tourist:- ***Both of you are from Bengal, right!***

Runa :- ***Yes! We are from Kolkata of West Bengal.***

A Gujarati Tourist:- ***Generally, Bengali tourists prefer to tour Andaman. We, the people of Western India prefer to tour Goa. I am from Surat of Gujarat. It's a very long way to Andaman for us; from Surat to Delhi and then from Delhi to Port Blair by flight. Anyway, enjoy yourselves. Ok.***

Arindam :- ***Ok.***

Runa :- ***Right now, we are in the right side of the Radhanagar Beach. Let us go towards the left side of the Radhanagar Beach. There is a very old Bhagwan Shiva Temple at the left side of the Radhanagar Beach.***

Arindam :- ***Byom Shankar! Chalo jaaoa jaak. Bhole Baba ke dekhe asi.***

****

Location: In front of Shiva Temple at Radhanagar Beach

*Arindam :- **After walking for around 10 minutes or so from the welcome gate of Radhanagar Beach, we have finally reached the Shiva Temple. This is a nearby village of Radhanagar Beach. At this place, we are feeling as if we are in a place like Bakkhali or Digha. Bakkhali beach also has the Goddess Bon-Bibi temple at its left side. Radhanagar beach also has the Bhagwan Shiva temple at its left side. A road is going somewhere from the left side of this Shiva Temple. It is leading towards a Radhakrishna Temple. Come on, let's go there also.***

*Runa :- **Ok!***

****

*Location: **In front of Radhakrishna Temple at Radhanagar Beach***

*Runa :- **This is a lovely place. This is a nursery of coconut trees. We are feeling as if we are in any village of Kerala. There is the Radhakrishna Temple.***

*Arindam :- **I have found out a small lane which goes towards the core area of village. We will walk through that lane.***

*Runa :- **No! No! I want to go back to the beach again and relax a bit.***

****

*Location: **On a wooden bench at Radhanagar Beach***

*Arindam :- **Aah! Ki thanda baataash! In this heated noon hours, this cool wind is really so refreshing.***

*Runa :- **See! That policeman is making an announcement.***

A policeman with microphone and mic:- ***All the tourists are hereby requested not to throw any plastics, plastic bottles or any other things on the beach. There are several dustbins kept in this beach. If we find any tourist throwing any things on the beach, then we may charge Rs. 500/- as a fine amount for polluting the beach. All the tourists who are bathing in this sea beach are requested not to go further, because, the undercurrent of this sea water is very strong. White and Yellow flags are hoisted at two ends of the beach. Please try to bath within the area between the flags at both ends. Don't bath in sea waters after consuming alcohol or any strong drugs. We hope that all our tourists are matured enough to co-operate with us. Thanks for visiting Radhanagar Beach. Enjoy your visit at Radhanagar Beach. Thank you.***

Arindam :- ***Don't take the administration of Radhanagar Beach too lightly. Administration is very strict out here. See there! A lifeboy is running towards the sea water with a tyre. By seeing the lifeboy running towards them, those half-drunkard young boys are coming towards the sea shore. Ha ha ha...I have seen this type of scene in 'Baywatch' TV serial only, where lifeguards run to save the people who are in danger while bathing in sea water.***

Runa :- ***Hmm. It is now 1.20 PM already. Let us go and have our lunch.***

****

Location: ***In front of a stall of coconuts at Radhanagar Beach***

Arindam :- ***Baah! After having a Bengali vegetarian meal, the coconut water is the best drink. I have finished drinking it up. Let me throw this coconut somewhere.***

Bengali seller of coconuts:- ***Na na dada! Eta Kolkata noy! Eta Havelock er Radhanagar! You are not allowed to throw coconut here and there. We have our own dustbin here. Please throw the***

coconut on this dustbin only. In this Island, we respect tourism. To maintain the beauty of this beach, we have to prevent any type of pollution from our end. Ei Radhanagar Beach nongra hoye gele, kono tourist aasbe naa. To maintain the profitability of our business, we need tourists and to retain tourists, we have to keep this Radhanagar Beach pollution free. It is as simple as that.

Runa :- ***Swaccha Bharat Abhijaan!***

Bengali seller of coconuts:- ***Exactly!***

Arindam :- ***See the fun! How the thinking strategies of any administrative power of any region can have an impact on the psychology of the people of that region. These guys are also Bengali people and the people who are in Digha are also Bengali people. But, due to good initiatives by the administration of Havelock Island, these Bengali people of Radhanagar Beach have understood the real brand value of a pollution free Sea Beach. Proshashan icche korle desh er unnati korte paare, abaar abanati o korte paare. Come on, the Maruti Van is standing there. Let us go inside it. It is already 2.20 PM.***

Runa :- ***Haan haan chalo.***

****

Location: ***Inside Maruti Van***

Arindam :- ***Is there any other beach which is famous in Havelock Island?***

Bengali Driver:- ***Yes, Kala Patthar Beach is also famous in this Island. From this Govindnagar, the road gets divided into two parts. One road is towards Radhanagar Beach and another road is towards Kala Patthar Beach.***

Arindam :- ***Oho! There is a branch of State Bank of India in Govindnagar! In my opinion, it is a better posting to get posted at Govindnagar Branch of Havelock Island rather than getting posted at Port Blair Branch for any officer of SBI.***

Bengali Driver:- ***No! Sir! This island is pleasant only in winter season. In summer season, it is too hot and humid. In rainy season, heavy downpours sometimes create too much problems. We have reached Havelock Island Jetty area. Can you see that MV Makruzz Office beside the Havelock Jetty Bus Stand?***

Arindam :- ***Yeah! Yeah!***

Bengali Driver:- ***Now, it is 2.45 PM. They will start the checking of MV Makruzz tickets at around 3 PM.***

Arindam :- ***So, your duty ends here. Bye! Bye!***

Bengali Driver:- ***Yes, Sir! Bye!***

****

Location: ***Havelock Island Jetty***

Arindam :- ***The staff of MV Makruzz office just gave a rubber stamp on our printed tickets. No fresh boarding passes this time. The red coloured Andaman Government buses start from this bus stand only to go to Radhanagar Beach.***

Runa :- ***We could have had our lunch here also. There are several restaurants here, both south Indian and Bengali. Look at the name of that restaurant, it is named as B3.***

Arindam :- ***B stands for Barbeque, B stands for Bar and B stands for Ball Dance. Therefore, it is B3. The sea waters near Havelock Jetty***

are so crystal clear. See, so many needle fishes are playing around. The fishermen are cooking some sea-fishes in their trawlers.

Runa :- ***Yeah! I am seeing it. Why the name of this island is Havelock Island?***

Arindam :- ***This island is named after a British General of East India Company. The name of that British General was Sir Henry Havelock. As because, this island has a name after a European, the European name also have its own impact to attract more European tourists in this island. Come on; let us relax a bit in the restroom of Havelock Island Jetty. It is only 3.05 PM. Still 25 minutes left to board the MV Makruzz.***

****

##

Episode – 06

*Location: **Inside the Restroom at Havelock Island Jetty***

*Mr. Tarua (A local resident of Havelock Island):- **How much is it costing per head to go from Havelock Jetty to Phoenix Bay Jetty by MV Makruzz?***

*Arindam :- **Rs. 975/- per head.***

*Mr. Tarua:- **Look at this Government Card and this ticket. They will take only Rs. 39/- from me on a government ferry boat.***

*Arindam :- **Are you a ghoti or a bangaal?***

*Mr. Tarua:- **My great grandfather was from Jessore. My grandfather migrated from Jessore to Bardhaman. Then, in 1971, when Indian Government under Indira Gandhi gave an offer to Bengali people to go and settle down in Andaman Islands, my grandfather accepted that offer. As a result, we are enjoying that facility. My grandfather and my father were government employee of Andaman Shipping Corporation and I am also a government employee of Andaman Shipping Corporation. I am a holder of Government Card which has lots of subsidies.***

*Runa :- **It is 3.20 PM now. Time to go now!***

*Arindam :- **Ok! Mr. Tarua, nice to meet you.***

*Mr. Tarua:- **Thik ache! Sujog pele abaar asbeen amader ei Havelock Island e.***

****

Location: Inside MV Makruzz Catamaran Ferry Boat

Arindam :- ***So many passengers of this ferry boat are vomiting now. The MV Makruzz is tilting too much while travelling on the deep sea water.***

A Staff of MV Makruzz:- ***This is a normal thing in this route. This is popularly known as Sea Sickness. In the morning, everyone had a light breakfast and at that time our journey was smooth because we were going downstream. Now, in this late afternoon, we are going upstream and it is high tide time also with lots of big waves in the sea water. As a result, MV Makruzz is tilting too much. As almost all passengers boarded the MV Makruzz after having a heavy lunch, they are feeling like vomiting or actually vomiting.***

Runa :- ***I am also feeling like vomiting again. Already, I vomited just a few moments ago in the washroom of this MV Makruzz.***

Arindam :- ***Ei re! Please give some paper bags. The passenger sitting beside me is also going to vomit.***

A staff of MV Makruzz:- ***Please take these paper bags and tissue papers. Madam, please tighten up the paper bags after vomiting on it. Please give a call to us. We are collecting these plastic bags from all the passengers and throwing it in the dustbin.***

Runa :- ***Ok!***

A staff of MV Makruzz:- ***Sir! Are you feeling uneasy also?***

Arindam :- ***No! No! I am enjoying this tilting ride. I never feel sea sickness.***

Security-in-charge of MV Makruzz:- ***Hey! Please play some videos of good hindi songs in the TV to divert the minds of passengers towards those songs.***

Another staff of MV Makruzz:- ***Yes! Sir!***

Arindam :- ***Bhuley jaao jeh tomaar bomi pacche. Just refresh your mind. Oi dekho, in the TV screen, A.R. Rahman is singing 'Dil se re' title track of 'DIL SE' film in an episode of MTV Coke Studio program.***

Runa :- ***Dil se re...dil se re. Yes, I am feeling good now.***

Arindam :- ***Ha ha ha. See, it's all in your mind. By seeing other passengers vomiting, your mind also felt like vomiting. That's why; the staffs of MV Makruzz are trying to divert the minds of passengers. The staffs of this Catamaran ferry boat are very smart and experienced indeed.***

Captain of MV Makruzz (announcing from his cabin):- ***Ladies and gentlemen, we hope that you had a nice journey with us. We are about to reach Phoenix Bay Jetty within 5 minutes. We hope that you will again choose to board our MV Makruzz in the near future. Thanks for boarding our MV Makruzz. Thank you.***

****

Location: ***Outside the main gate of Phoenix Bay Jetty area***

North Bihari Driver:- ***Aaiye Sir! The Tata Sumo car has been parked there. You had a nice journey, Sir?***

Arindam :- ***Haan haan. The journey was good. We liked the Havelock Island.***

****

Location: ***Inside the dining room of Palm Grove Eco Resort***

*Arindam :- **The chef of this Palm Grove Eco Resort takes a long time to cook foods but never compromises with quality. The Chicken chowmein is really delicious. A plate of Chicken chowmein costs Rs. 150/-, but look at the quantity of chowmein. Both of us are sharing it, still, we are having a hard time to finish it up. A nice Chinese dinner indeed!***

*Runa :- **If we consider the quantity of Chicken chowmein, then Rs. 150/- is quite a reasonable price. Even 3 persons can share and eat one plate of Chicken chowmein. What's our plan for tomorrow?***

*Arindam :- **Tomorrow, we will go to Ross Island, if possible to North Bay Island also in the morning. In the afternoon, if we get time, then we may visit Chidiya Tapu. But, tomorrow, we will not book any car from this resort. The car booking is somewhat expensive. We will go by local auto-rickshaws only.***

*Runa :- **Ok.***

****

*Location: **Brichgunj Chowk at Port Blair***

*Arindam :- **Auto! We want to go to Aberdeen Jetty from here? How much?***

*A Tamil Auto-rickshaw driver:- **120 rupees, Sir!***

*Arindam :- **Ok! Come on, sit inside the Auto-Rickshaw.***

*Runa :- **This ice-cream of 'Jamai' company is so delicious! I love this Vanilla taste.***

*Arindam :- **Mine is butter scotch flavour. Daarao, ekta confusion clear kori. Accha! Woh Aberdeen Jetty se Ross Island jaane ke liye boat chorhta hain kya?***

A Tamil auto-rickshaw driver:- ***Oho! Aap ko Ross Island jaana hain. Ek minute, mere ko bhi confusion hain. Ek phone kar leta hoon apne dost ko. Hello! Suriya Bhai! Main Manishankar! Accha ek baat batao, woh Ross Island jaanewala boat kahan se chorhta hain abhi? Aberdeen Jetty ya Junglighat Jetty?***

Suriya (A Tour operator cum friend of that Auto-rickshaw driver):- ***Subha ko, Junglighat Jetty se chorhta hain. Shaam ko, Aberdeen Jetty se?***

A Tamil auto-rickshaw driver:- ***We have to go to Junglighat Jetty, Sir. Don't worry; the fare is 120 rupees only. After Tsunami in 26th December 2004, Junglighat Jetty was totally destroyed. Again, the Andaman Government created another jetty in Junglighat. After Tsunami, Ferry boats used to go from Aberdeen Jetty only to Ross Island. But, now, the ferry boats go to Ross Island from Junglighat Jetty also. Aberdeen Jetty is in the north-eastern side of South Andaman Island and Junglighat Jetty is in the north-western side of South Andaman Island. Ross Island is nearer from Aberdeen Jetty.***

Arindam :- ***Ok. Now it is 8.15 AM. We will get ferry boats, naah? After visiting Ross Island, will we get time to go to Chidiya Tapu?***

A Tamil auto-rickshaw driver:- ***Of course, Sir! All ferry boats start from 8.30 AM itself. But, you will not get time to go to Chidiya Tapu after visiting Ross Island, North Bay Island and Viper Island. Anyway, in Chidiya Tapu, tourists go to see the sunset only and some beautiful birds. Kitne din ke tour mein aaye hain saab?***

Arindam :- ***4 days tour. This is our last day of tour.***

A Tamil auto-rickshaw driver:- ***Kahan kahan ghuma, Sir?***

Arindam :- ***Cellular Jail, Wandoor Beach, Baratang Island and Havelock Island.***

A Tamil auto-rickshaw driver:- ***Havelock Island aap ko accha laaga, Sir?***

Arindam :- ***It's good but quite expensive!***

A Tamil auto-rickshaw driver:- ***Exactly! 10 or 15 years back, the people of Havelock Island used to come in Port Blair in search of jobs. But, now, due to foreign tourists, that Havelock Island has got developed rapidly. Aab ush Havelock Island ke logon ko thoda jyaada hee ghamand ho gaya hain. Arrey Bhai! You the people of Havelock Island are charging too much money from foreign tourists that are ok. But, when the local people of Andaman are visiting Havelock Island, they are also charging the same price from us. Sir, you may take it otherwise. But, we, the Tamil people really understand the value of money and we know how hard it is to earn money. Kisi ke paash paise ke pedh nahi hota hain. I went to Havelock Island last year with my family members. In a restaurant, they charged 200 rupees for a vegetarian thali. That vegetarian thali costs only 60 rupees in Port Blair. Woh vegetarian thali kya sona chaandi se taiyaar kiya tha? Woh vegetarian thali bhi toh chawaal se hee banaa tha. Inflation is created by human beings only but at the end of the day, everyone blames the Indian Government.***

Arindam :- ***Ha ha ha...Well said. But, yes, Havelock Island is somewhat an over-hyped place. Maybe, corals are good in Havelock Island or maybe in Neil Island.***

A Tamil auto-rickshaw driver:- ***No, Sir! Corals are best in North Bay Island. Today, you must visit North Bay Island and see those sea corals. Lijiye saab, aa gaya Junglighat Jetty. This is the ticket counter. You will get tickets for Ross Island, North Bay Island and Viper Island from here only.***

Arindam :- ***Thank you for giving us proper information, otherwise we would have gone to Aberdeen Jetty. Take these 120 rupees.***

****

Location: ***In front of ticket counter at Junglighat Jetty***

A staff of Junglighat Jetty:- ***Sir! Please remember your boat name. It is MV Nandini. The ticket price is Rs. 550/- per head. In total, it is Rs. 1100/-. Here is your ticket. Please wait inside the waiting room. A person will call out by the boat name. At that time, you must proceed towards the Jetty ghat to board on MV Nandini.***

Arindam :- ***Ok!***

****

Location: ***Inside the waiting room of Junglighat Jetty***

Arindam :- ***By seeing the surrounding area of this Junglighat Jetty, you can have an idea that this place was badly affected due to the Tsunami in 2004.***

Runa :-***Yeah! That's true!***

A female staff of Jolly Buoy Scuba Diving Firm:- ***Good morning, Sir! Good morning, Madam! Would you like to go for Scuba Diving in North Bay Island? You can see the colourful world under the sea water. Even you can feed the fishes with your own hand. Total time is of 60 minutes. We will give you 15 minutes training. If you are ok with training, then only you can go for real scuba diving for 45 minutes under the water. We will also make a Video CD of yours and hand it over to you. The total cost for Scuba Diving is Rs. 2500/- per person inclusive of Video CD charges.***

Arindam :- ***Baba! Bole ki goh? 2500 taaka per head. Oto paisa toh anini.***

A female staff of Jolly Buoy Scuba Diving Firm:- ***Chesta kore dekhte paaren, Sir! Jinish taa khub ee bhalo.***

Arindam :- ***Oh! Aapni bangaali. Ki surname apnaar? Baari kothay?***

A female staff of Jolly Buoy Scuba Diving Firm:- ***Amar title mondal. Baari Wandoor e? Wandoor e gachen?***

Arindam :- ***Haan, gechi.***

A female staff of Jolly Buoy Scuba Diving Firm:- ***Ok. Then Sir, keep this leaflet with you to give any reference about our firm to your friends or relatives so that they can enjoy scuba diving if they ever visit to Andaman.***

Arindam :- ***Yeah! Sure! Sure! Ei kagaj taa rekhe daao dekhi tomaar kaache. You can give reference to someone.***

Runa :- ***Ok.***

A female staff of Jolly Buoy Scuba Diving Firm:- ***Ok! Sir! Thanks for listening.***

Arindam :- ***Ok.***

Runa :- ***That person is calling our boat name.***

A staff of Junglighat Jetty:- ***The passengers of MV Nandini ferry boat are hereby requested to proceed towards the jetty ghat to board the MV Nandini ferry boat.***

Arindam :- ***Chalo! chalo!***

****

Location: Inside MV Nandini ferry boat

1st lifeboy of MV Nandini ferry boat:- ***Please don't click photos of the area that you are seeing on your right side. That's the naval area of Port Blair. As per the strict orders from Indian Navy, no one is allowed to click photos of the naval area of Port Blair. Indian Navy may take strict actions on tourists and staffs of any boat, if their orders are violated.***

A passenger of MV Nandini ferry boat:- ***Oho! Sorry! I was not aware of those orders. I will not click any photos of that naval area.***

****

A Bengali passenger of MV Nandini ferry boat:- ***Oi dekho, Chatham Island. That's the Chatham Bridge! That bridge connects the Chatham Island with the South Andaman Island.***

A Jat (from Himachal Pradesh) passenger of MV Nandini ferry boat:- ***Actually, the development of Port Blair started from this Chatham Island only. Lieutenant Archibald Blair of East India Company came to this Chatham Island and planned to open a timber saw mill to utilize the trees of the forest in Chatham Island. Even the Chatham Bridge was initially made of timber. That is, it was around 100 metres long wooden bridge only. Later on, East India Company shifted their colony further deeper in South Andaman Island and named it as Port Blair because some local people of Chatham Islands started revolting against the British colonies in Chatham Island. Chatham Saw Mill was becoming one of the best revenue earning centre for East India Company. That's why; during 2nd World War, the Japanese ships bombarded Chatham Saw Mill and also destroyed the Chatham Bridge. Still, the Chatham Saw Mill has not lost its glory. The Chatham Bridge was rebuilt again.***

****

Arindam :- ***See, the staffs of MV Nandini ferry boat are trying to catch a big fish. They have tied a coloured plastic fish of small size with the big bait. The bait is tied with a very long wire connected with this boat. As the boat progresses, the coloured plastic fish also looks like a swimming coloured fish in the sea water. If by chance, any big sea fish tries to eat or gulp that coloured plastic fish and get stuck with the bait, then it's a gala treat for these fishermen.***

Runa :- ***It is not so easy to catch a big fish like that. Big fishes are always big fishes and are very smart.***

2nd lifeboy of MV Nandini Boat:- ***We have reached Ross Island. You can remove life jacket from your body and proceed towards Ross Island. Now, it is 10.50 AM. Please come back to this Jetty ghat at 11.30 AM. Ross Island was named after Sir Daniel Ross, a European mariner. Ross Island was the base island or the headquarter island of British Government. Later on, Japanese took control of this Ross Island. Even Indian flag was hoisted at this Ross Island by Netaji Subhashchandra Bose. You can also see the Japanese Bunkers just before the entry gate of Ross Island. After an earthquake, this Ross Island became a deserted island. There are no human habitats here. Though, some animals have been kept in the small reserve forest area of this island. The entire Ross Island is now under the control of Indian Navy. There is a guest house of Indian Navy in Ross Island. Light and Sound show is also conducted in Ross Island. Every day, the ferry boat services start at late afternoon around 3.30 PM from Aberdeen Jetty to come to Ross Island. In the evening, tourists enjoy the Light and Sound show in Ross Island and then go back to Aberdeen Jetty by ferry boat. Ok! Go and enjoy the Ross Island.***

A matured married Bengali woman tourist:- ***Ne! Toraa toh ekhanei 5 minute borbaad kore dili. Ei gulo toh nouka cholakaalin bolte paartis.***

3rd lifeboy of MV Nandini Boat:- ***Thik ache boudi! We will start at 11.35 AM.***

Arindam :- ***Ha ha ha...MV Nandini naam suneyi sandeho hoyechilo. Ekhan sandeho clear holo. Look at that name plate inside the boat. Owner of MV Nandini is a Bangladeshi Muslim. The license of this boat has to be renewed on the June month of 2016. This boat is having 5 lifeboys, 1 sailor and 1 engineer. In total, 7 staffs. They are part-time fishermen too.***

Runa :- ***Thik ache chalo. By reading too many detective books, you are always curious about anything and generally start doubting on strangers. Let us now visit Ross Island.***

****

Episode – 07

Location: Ross Island

Arindam :- ***Each and every building is of red colour in this Ross Island. It can be termed as Red Ross Island. Even the barricades are red coloured too. British people were too obsessed with red colour it seems. Aha! I can see***

Japanese Bunkers! Wait! I will stand in front of the Japanese bunkers with an umbrella above my head. You just click my photo. The letters, 'JAPANESE BUNKERS' should also come in the photo.

Runa :- ***Ok! Ok! I have clicked your photo! What a weird pose! That umbrella will save the Japanese bunkers from the nuclear bombs discharged from American fighter planes or what!***

Arindam :- ***Ha ha ha. Actually, to make the letters, 'JAPANESE BUNKERS' prominent in the photo, I used that umbrella in this too sunny morning.***

Runa :- ***Satyi, tomaar ki buddhi. Uuh! Oi dekho! In the ticket counter, it is written that entry fee per person is Rs. 50/- and camera fee is Rs. 20/-. For video photography, the fee is Rs. 40/-.***

Arindam :- ***Ok! Two entry tickets and one camera! Total 120 rupees.***

A computer operator at the ticket counter of Ross Island:- ***Ok! Sir! Welcome to Ross Island.***

Arindam :- ***Thank you! Koi goh! Chalo Ross Island er bhetore jaai ebaar.***

****

*Runa :- **Wow! A deer is licking those coconut shells and tourists are rubbing the deer's head and skin. Let me click a photo of that deer.***

*Arindam :- **Harin o narkol saansh khete bhalobashe dekhchi. Dyakho tumi amar gaan geye boso naa, 'Amar sona r harin chaai, amar sona r harin chaai, toraa je jaa bolish bhai.'***

*Runa :- **Ha ha ha...dhaath, tumi na; satyi baba, paaro o botey. Come on; let us go towards the Church.***

*Arindam :- **Such a beautiful Island! British people really made this island so beautiful, but, alas, Japanese people and Mother Nature had some other plans for them.***

****

*Arindam :- **We have seen Bakery House, Chief Commissioner's House. He he he...see! A deer is standing in front of a small lane and some tourists are touching its forehead. That deer with long horns is trying to attack the tourists. Now, that deer is going through that small lane. This must be the middle portion of the island. Come on, let us follow this deer.***

*Runa :- **Why are you wasting so much time on that deer, I really don't understand.***

****

*Arindam :- **See! Where we have come after following this deer! A big pond in the middle of this Ross Island! Maybe, this is was the swimming pool of British people. All the deer are eating some grasses beside that red coloured house. Let us see what is there inside this house. Oho! Nice red house with a white coloured door and glassed window. See, I can see two beds, some chairs and tables.***

*Runa :- **Do you want to stay in this house or what?***

*Arindam :- **Aaha! Jodi satyi ee thakte partum! But, not a single tourist is allowed to stay here. Maybe, there are ghosts inside this house. All the British ghosts!***

*Runa :- **Dhaath! Amar ebaar bhoy laagche! Kothao kono lokjan nei, nirjan sunsaan elaaka. Tar opor abaar bhooth er bhoy dekhaccho. Come on, let us go from here.***

*Arindam :- **See! You are shouting at me and by hearing your shouting, those 3 deer are standing in front of us and staring at us. Ei toraa dekhchish toh, toder boudi kamon amaake bokche. Ami toh ekhaane thakbo bolei esechilum.***

*An old deer (made a deep breathing sound while nodding his head and staring at two human beings):- **Phurrh.***

*Runa :- **Ha ha ha...Come on; let us go near the Ross Island Jetty as it is 10.25 AM already.***

****

*Arindam :- **There are too many coconut trees in this Ross Island, but, what is more fascinating here is that some coconut trees are crooked ones. As if, these coconut trees has grown up by doing some break dancing. Aha! A person is selling Kheer kulfi malai at Rs. 20/- each. Kulfi malai khaabe?***

*Runa :- **Yes! Buy two Kheer kulfi malai. It's too hot out here.***

****

*Location: **Inside MV Nandini ferry boat***

4th Lifeboy of MV Nandini ferry boat:- ***So, all the 28 passengers of the boat have come back. Kato re? 28 hoyeche?***

An engineer of MV Nandini ferry boat:- ***Haan, counting kore niyechi. Athaash jon ee ache.***

4th Lifeboy of MV Nandini ferry boat:- ***Ok! We will now start our journey towards North Bay Island.***

****

A matured married Bengali woman tourist:- ***I have spotted a peacock. The peacock was hiding behind a bush beside the lane which was going towards a beach side in Ross Island. You sat on a bench after feeling tired, but, I walked towards that beach and came back.***

Husband of a matured married Bengali woman tourist:- ***Oh! ekebaare biswa jay kore felecho jyano! Ami mayur er daak sunte peyechilam botey, kintu darshan paaini. Anyway, I have spotted lots of desi hens, desi ducks and squirrels.***

****

5th Lifeboy of MV Nandini ferry boat:- ***We have reached North Bay Island. As there are sea corals in North Bay Island, the ferry boats are not allowed to go near the shallow waters of island. You can see a floating pavement has been created from the region of deep waters to the region of shallow waters. You have to get down at the floating pavement and walk towards the North Bay Island. You are not supposed to remove your life jacket until and unless you reach the North Bay Island.***

Sailor of MV Nandini ferry boat:- ***In this North Bay Island, you can see sea corals by 4 ways; Glass boating, snorkelling, scuba diving and sea walks. Only in glass boating, you don't have to wet your***

clothes. For glass boating, it is only Rs. 300/- per head which is much cheaper. In glass boating only, you can see sea corals of 7 important points in the waters of North Bay Island. If anyone of you is interested in glass boating, then give 300 rupees per head to me. I will arrange a glass boat immediately and you will see sea corals even before landing on North Bay Island. In the glass boat, we will cover the boat with a big cloth at the top, so that you can take photos and videos of sea corals through the glasses of the glass boat. Dijiye, 300 rupees kar ke dijiye!

Arindam :- ***Take these 600 rupees for two heads.***

****

Location: ***On the Glass boat at North Bay Island***

Sailor of Glass boat:- ***See! Now, we are at a point where you can see deep sea corals and some colourful fishes hovering around it.***

Runa :- ***Daarun! Daarun! Sea corals are so beautiful!***

Arindam :- ***You click the photos of corals with your mobile handset. I will take the videos of sea corals with my digital camera.***

Sailor of Glass boat:- ***Now, we are at a point where you can see sea corals which looks like human brains.***

Arindam :- ***Really amazing! We are feeling as if someone has thrown some human brains on the sea bed.***

Sailor of Glass boat:- ***The glass boating ends here. We will drop you all at that floating pavement now. It is 12.30 PM now. You, the passengers of MV Nandini ferry boat must reach near the floating pavement at 2.30 PM.***

****

Location: In North Bay Island

*Runa :- **The 20 minutes glass boating was really awesome. We will not go for snorkelling, scuba diving and sea walks. Then, how will we spend our time here?***

*Arindam :- **Wait! Let me take out a 20 rupees note. On the backside of this 20 rupees note, can you see the picture of a lighthouse? This is the North Point lighthouse of North Bay Island. As North Bay Island is popular worldwide for its lovely and beautiful sea corals, the Indian Government decided to print a picture of North Point Lighthouse on this 20 rupees note. Come on; let us walk towards that North Point Lighthouse. The road is somewhat steep as it is on a hillock and the distance is just 265 metres from the floating pavement of North Bay Island.***

*Runa :- **Please buy a bottle of cold drinks. It is too hot and while walking towards that Lighthouse, we may feel thirsty.***

*Arindam :- **We already have some cold drinks of Sprite in this bottle. Wait! Let me buy a coconut for 20 rupees and tell that owner of coconut stall to pour the coconut water in this empty water bottle. Coconut water is better than cold drinks.***

****

Location: Inside the premises of North Point Lighthouse

*Runa :- **Uuh! It is too hot here in this afternoon. See, a North Indian couple is already resting at a halfway mark of this 265 meters long pavement. Both of them were inside MV Nandini ferry boat.***

*A male tourist from Delhi:- **Kya garmi hain bhai! Thoda rest le lete hain. Aap log chaliye, hum log aate hain.***

Arindam :- ***Thik hain!***

****

Location: ***A small hut (open at all ends) in front of North Point Lighthouse***

Arindam :- ***This lighthouse is really too tall. Earlier, maybe, there were permits to climb at the top of the lighthouse.***

Runa :- ***Climbing at the top of lighthouse in this hot season. Babah! Kono dorkaar nei.***

Wife of the male tourist from Delhi:- ***Ha ha ha...sahi mein, kaun ish garmi mein lighthouse ke upar jaayega!***

Runa :- ***But, the view towards the Sea water from this point is just fabulous. There are coconut trees and other trees on both sides. Through the middle of those trees, you can see the sea water. Even I can see a MV Makruzz sailing on the sea water. Let me click a photo of this entire scenery.***

Arindam :- ***I have seen the photo of this scenic view in a calendar also.***

A male tourist from Delhi:- ***Haan haan, bahut saare calendar mein yeh scenic beauty ka photo hain.***

Runa :- ***Time to go now. It is already 1.20 PM. We have to do our lunch also.***

Arindam :- ***Aap log kya baad mein aayenge?***

Wife of the male tourist from Delhi:- ***We already had our lunch. We have a packed program today. Again in the afternoon, we will come to Ross Island from Aberdeen Jetty. As per our tour operator's***

schedule, we have to see the Light and Sound show of Ross Island too.

Arindam :- ***Oh! Ok!***

A male tourist from Delhi:- ***Actually, humre tour operator bewakoof banaa diya. Agar Ross Island mein light and sound show dekhne jaana hee hain ekbaar, toh phir subah mein Ross Island ghumake extra tour costing karne ka kya jaroorat hain?***

Arindam :- ***Ha ha ha. If tour operators will not do profits, then what will they eat? Anyway, see you both in MV Nandini ferry boat again. Bye.***

****

Location: ***Inside a restaurant of North Bay Island***

Owner of restaurant in North Bay Island:- ***Ki khaaben bolun, Sir! Fried Rice, Chicken biriyani, Chilli Chicken, Chicken Chowmein.***

Arindam :- ***Paati daal, bhaath ar sabji hobe ki?***

Owner of restaurant in North Bay Island:- ***Hobe Sir! Vegetarian thali per plate is 120 rupees only.***

Arindam :- ***Taai daao dekhi.***

****

Location: ***Inside MV Nandini Boat***

Arindam :- ***The colour of this sea water changes. In the morning, it was of different colour and now in this late afternoon, it is deep bluish. Such a romantic colour of sea water!***

*Runa :- **Accha! Almost all the trainers for scuba diving in North Bay Island were mongoloid people. Were they Nepali or Chinese or North-East Indian?***

*Arindam :- **If I am not so wrong, they were of Burmese origin. Myanmar is not too far from here. People of Burma are also of mongoloid origin.***

****

*Engineer of MV Nandini Boat:- **We have reached Viper Island. Don't go deeper into this island. The forest of this island is very dangerous and full of poisonous snakes. Just see the court room and the hanging house at the top of that hillock. Sher Ali Afridi was hanged at that hanging house. Earlier, British people also had a jail in this island. This was the island of vipers, the deadly poisonous snakes. But, many historians are of the opinion that this island is named after Lieutenant Archibald Blair's vessel, Viper. Whatever it maybe, just visit this island within 15 minutes.***

****

Location: On the Viper Island

*Husband of a matured married Bengali woman tourist:- **When the decision always taken by British Government was to hang an Indian prisoner in this Viper Island, then what was the essence of constructing a court house in this island? Bichaar toh kichui hoto naa, sudhui faanshi r sajaa hoto. Jato sab lok dekhano r jonne, ekta court house khule rekhechilo.***

*A matured Bengali woman tourist:- **Ha ha ha...***

*Arindam :- **This Viper Island is just at the opposite side of Junglighat Jetty. I can hear some sounds from the jungle. Maybe, there are elephants in this jungle.***

Runa :- ***Maybe! Because I can see several big heaps of potty which are quite similar to the potty we see in a cage of elephant in any zoo. Chalo! Chalo! Let us go back to the ferry boat.***

****

Location: ***Inside MV Nandini ferry boat***

Sailor of MV Nandini ferry boat:- ***We have reached Junglighat Jetty. We hope that you have enjoyed the journey. Please visit Andaman again. Thank you.***

All the passengers of MV Nandini ferry boat:- ***Thank you.***

****

Location: ***Outside Prothrapur Jail***

Arindam :- ***There is nothing so historical about this jail. This has been constructed by Indian Government only. But, this big tree outside the gate of Prothrapur Jail looks quite historical. It's a very old tree indeed.***

Runa :- ***Let us now go back to our resort which is just at a 5 minutes walking distance from here.***

****

Location: ***Inside the Dining Hall of Palm Grove Eco Resort***

Arindam :- ***Baah! This Andamani Biriyani for 150 rupees per plate is delicious. The quantity is so much that 2 persons can easily eat it by sharing. No rose water and potato in this biriyani. There is curry patta, elaichi, kaaju badam and kissmiss. Chicken pieces are very well roasted. It has a different taste, but, quite delicious. Isn't it so?***

Can you cook biriyani at house? Oh! To whom I am saying! You don't even know the letter 'C' of cooking. It is so shameful to have a wife who doesn't know how to cook food.

Runa :- ***I am trying to learn cooking. I have never cooked any food as of now.***

Arindam :- ***Learn it fast. Generally, an Indian man doesn't give too much love and respect to that Indian woman who doesn't know cooking, no matter whether she is a working woman or a housewife. If you don't learn cooking, then it may hamper our marriage relationship in long run. Uuh!***

****

Location: ***Inside Spicejet plane at Port Blair Airport***

Captain of Spicejet flight:- ***Welcome to SG254 flight of Spicejet. Please fasten up your seat belts. We are about to start our journey towards Kolkata within a few minutes. Thank you.***

Runa :- ***I will make a video through the window when this flight will take off from Port Blair Airport.***

Arindam :- ***Ok! The name of that video will be 'Bye! Bye! Port Blair!' as we have completed our "ANDAMAN TOUR OF 2016."***

****

THE END

Printed by Libri Plureos GmbH in Hamburg,
Germany